LA GRANGE
PUBLIC LIBRARY

10 West Cossitt Avenue
La Grange, IL 60525
lagrangelibrary.org   708.352.0576

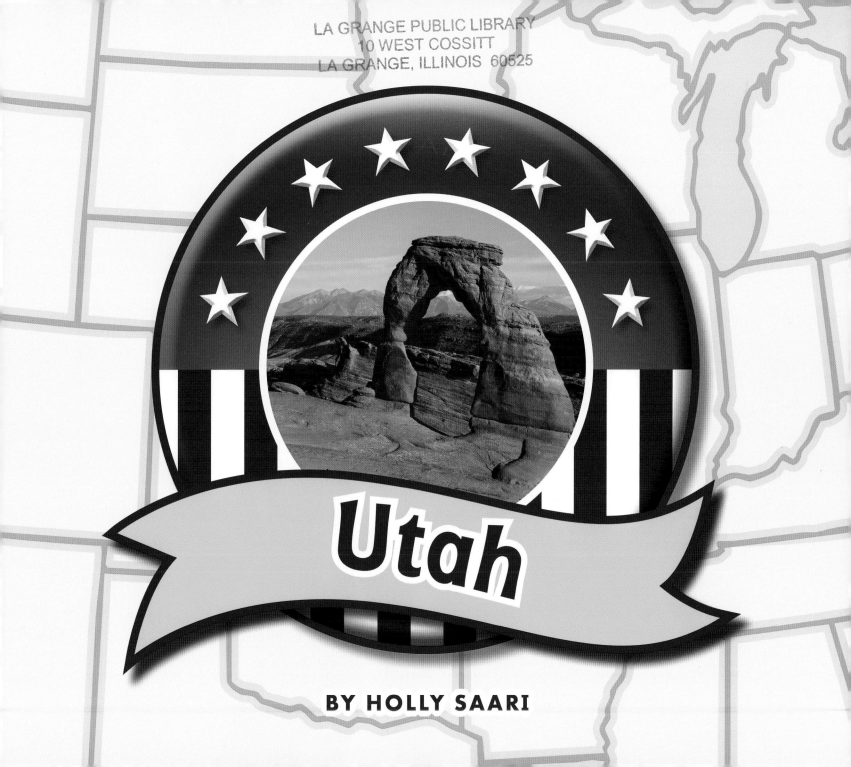

Utah

BY HOLLY SAARI

J
979.2
SAA

DEC 2012

Published by The Child's World®
1980 Lookout Drive • Mankato, MN 56003-1705
800-599-READ • www.childsworld.com

ACKNOWLEDGMENTS
The Child's World®: Mary Berendes, Publishing Director
The Design Lab: Design and production
Red Line Editorial: Editorial direction

PHOTO CREDITS: Scott Prokop/Shutterstock Images, cover, 1, 3; Matt Kania/
Map Hero, Inc., 4, 5; iStockphoto, 7; Kushch Dmitry/Shutterstock Images, 9;
123RF, 10; Werner Bollmann/Photolibrary, 11; Shutterstock Images, 13; North
Wind Picture Archives/Photolibrary, 15; Carolyn Kaster/AP Images, 17; Peter
Kramer/AP Images, 19; Michael Madsen/iStockphoto, 21; One Mile Up, 22;
Quarter-dollar coin image from the United States Mint, 22

$27.07

LIBRARY OF CONGRESS CATALOGING-IN-PUBLICATION DATA
Saari, Holly.
  Utah / by Holly Saari.
     p. cm.
  Includes bibliographical references and index.
  ISBN 978-1-60253-489-6 (library bound : alk. paper)
  1. Utah—Juvenile literature. I. Title.

F826.3.S23 2010
979.2—dc22

2010019329

Printed in the United States of America in Mankato, Minnesota.
July 2010
F11538

On the cover:
Arches National
Park is near
Moab, Utah.

CONTENTS

Geography

Let's explore Utah! Utah is in the western United States.

IDAHO

WYOMING

• Promontory

• Brigham City

Great Salt Lake

•Ogden

Wasatch Mountains

★
Salt Lake City

Tooele •

NEVADA

•Provo

UTAH

Rocky Mountains

Richfield •

Arches National Park
• Moab

COLORADO

Monticello •

St. George •

ARIZONA

NEW MEXICO

NORTH
WEST — EAST
SOUTH

Cities

Salt Lake City is the capital of Utah. It is the state's largest city. Provo is another large city in the state.

Salt Lake City is near the Wasatch Mountains. ▶

Land

The Rocky Mountains are in northeast Utah. Other areas of the state have **canyons** and **valleys**. Wind and rain have formed large rocks into **arches** in parts of Utah. Deserts cover one-third of the state. The Great Salt Lake is in Utah. It is the largest saltwater lake in the western **hemisphere**.

The Rocky Mountains range is the largest system of mountains in North America.

This arch is in Arches National Park. ▶

Plants and Animals

Less than one-third of Utah has forests. Its state tree is the blue spruce. The state flower is the sego lily. Lizards and snakes live in Utah's dry deserts. The state also has coyotes and deer. The state bird is the California seagull.

The sego lily can grow well in desert areas. ▶

People and Work

About 2.8 million people live in Utah. Most of the people live in large cities. Many people work in mines. Copper, coal, gold, and silver are all mined in Utah. Oil is another important product here. Other people work in **tourism**. They help visitors to the state. Many people come to Utah to ski.

Farmers in Utah raise cattle.

Kennecott Copper Mine is the largest copper mine in the world. ▶

13

History

Native Americans have lived in this area for thousands of years. In the 1700s, people from Spain came to the area. Later, Mormons wanted to practice their **religion** in peace. They traveled from the eastern United States to the Utah area in the 1800s. Mexico owned the land at this time. Then the United States won the land in a war. Utah became the forty-fifth state on January 4, 1896.

Brigham Young led Mormons to the Utah area. ▶

Ways of Life

The Mormon religion is important in Utah. The religion is also called the Church of Jesus Christ of Latter-day Saints. Salt Lake City is a center for the religion. The Sundance Film **Festival** is held in the state each year. Actors and directors come to see new movies.

The Winter Olympics were held in Salt Lake City in 2002.

The Sundance Film Festival is held in Park City, Utah. ▶

Famous People

Singers Donny and Marie Osmond were born and live in Utah. Writer Bernard De Voto was also born in Utah. He wrote stories about the West. He won awards for his history writing.

Siblings Donny and Marie Osmond had their ▶ own television show in the 1970s.

Famous Places

The Great Salt Lake is a **popular** place to visit. The lake's water is saltier than ocean water. The Salt Lake **Tabernacle** is well known for its large organ. It is home to the Mormon Tabernacle Choir.

The Great Salt Lake is about 75 miles (121 km) long and about 35 miles (56 km) wide. ▶

State Symbols

Seal

The beehive on Utah's state seal stands for hard work. Go to **childsworld.com/links** for a link to Utah's state Web site, where you can get a firsthand look at the state seal.

Flag

The bald eagle on Utah's flag is the national bird of the United States.

Quarter

Utah's state quarter shows a train. In 1869, two railroads joined in Promontory, Utah. This connected the eastern and western United States. The quarter came out in 2007.

Glossary

arches (ARCH-ez): Arches are curved structures. Wind and rain have formed large rocks into arches in parts of Utah.

canyons (KAN-yunz): Canyons are deep valleys that often have rivers running through them. Utah has canyons.

festival (FESS-tih-vul): A festival is a celebration for an event or holiday. An important film festival is held in Utah each year.

hemisphere (HEM-iss-feer): A hemisphere is a half of Earth. Utah's Great Salt Lake is the largest saltwater lake in the western hemisphere.

popular (POP-yuh-lur): To be popular is to be enjoyed by many people. The Great Salt Lake is a popular place to visit in Utah.

religion (reh-LIJ-un): Religion is a system of beliefs about God or gods. Many people in Utah belong to the Church of Jesus Christ of Latter-day Saints, also called the Mormon religion.

seal (SEEL): A seal is a symbol a state uses for government business. Utah's seal shows a beehive to stand for hard work.

symbols (SIM-bulz): Symbols are pictures or things that stand for something else. The seal and the flag are Utah's symbols.

tabernacle (TAB-ur-nak-ul): A tabernacle is a place of worship. The Salt Lake Tabernacle is in Utah.

tourism (TOOR-ih-zum): Tourism is visiting another place (such as a state or country) for fun or the jobs that help these visitors. Tourism is popular in Utah.

valleys (VAL-eez): Valleys are the low points between two mountains. Utah has valleys.

Further Information

Books

Hall, Becky. *A is for Arches: A Utah Alphabet*. Chelsea, MI: Sleeping Bear Press, 2003.

Keller, Laurie. *The Scrambled States of America*. New York: Henry Holt, 2002.

Thornton, Brian. *The Everything Kids' States Book: Wind Your Way Across Our Great Nation*. Avon, MA: Adams Media, 2007.

Web Sites

Visit our Web site for links about Utah: *childsworld.com/links*

Note to Parents, Teachers, and Librarians: We routinely verify our Web links to make sure they are safe and active sites. So encourage your readers to check them out!

Index